Karl Marx
The Usefulness of Crime

ERIS
gems

A PHILOSOPHER PRODUCES IDEAS, a poet poems, a clergyman sermons, a professor compendia and so on. A criminal produces crimes. If we look a little closer at the connection between this latter branch of production and society as a whole, we shall rid ourselves of many prejudices. The criminal produces not only crimes but also criminal law, and with this also the professor who gives lectures on criminal law and in addition to this the inevitable compendium in which this same professor throws his lectures onto the general market as 'commodities'. This brings with it augmentation of national wealth, quite apart from the personal enjoyment which—as a competent Witness, Herr Professor Roscher, [tells] us—the manuscript of the compendium brings to its originator himself.

The criminal moreover produces the whole of the police and of criminal justice, constables, judges, hangmen, juries, etc.; and all these different lines of business, which form equally many categories of the social division of labour, develop different capacities of the human spirit, create new needs and new ways of satisfying them. Torture alone has given rise to the most ingenious mechanical inventions, and employed many honourable craftsmen in the production of its instruments.

The criminal produces an impression, partly moral and partly tragic, as the case may be, and in this way renders a 'service' by arousing the moral and aesthetic feelings of the public. He produces not only compendia on Criminal Law, not only penal codes and along with them legislators in this field, but also art, *belles-lettres*, novels, and even tragedies, as not only Müllner's *Schuld* and Schiller's *Räuber* show, but also [Sophocles'] *Oedipus* and [Shakespeare's] *Richard the Third*. The criminal breaks the monotony and everyday security of bourgeois life. In this way he keeps it from stagnation, and gives rise to that uneasy tension and agility without which even the spur of competition would get blunted. Thus he gives a stimulus to the productive forces. While crime takes a part of the superfluous population off the labour market and thus reduces competition among the labourers—up to a certain point preventing wages from falling below the minimum—the struggle against crime absorbs another part of this population. Thus the criminal comes in as one of those natural 'counterweights' which bring about a correct balance and open up a whole perspective of 'useful' occupations.

The effects of the criminal on the development of productive power can be shown in detail. Would locks ever have reached their present degree of excellence had there been no thieves? Would the making of bank-notes have reached its present perfection had there been no forgers? Would the microscope have found its way into the sphere of ordinary commerce (see Babbage) but for trading frauds? Doesn't practical chemistry owe just as much to adulteration of commodities and the efforts to show it up as to the honest zeal for production?

Crime, through its constantly new methods of attack on property, constantly calls into being new methods of defence, and so is as productive as strikes for the invention of machines. And if one leaves the sphere of private crime: would the world-market ever have come into being but for national crime? Indeed, would even the nations have arisen? And hasn't the Tree of Sin been at the same time the Tree of Knowledge ever since the time of Adam?

In his *Fable of the Bees* (1705) Mandeville had already shown that every possible kind of occupation is productive, and had given expression to the line of this whole argument:

> "That what we call Evil in this World, Moral as well as Natural, is the grand Principle that makes us Sociable Creatures, the solid Basis, the *Life and Support of all Trades and Employments* without exception [...] there we must look for the true origin of all Arts and Sciences; and [...] the moment, Evil

ceases, the Society must he spoil'd if not totally dissolve'd".

Only Mandeville was of course infinitely bolder and more honest than the philistine apologists of bourgeois society.

ERIS

265 Riverside Dr.
New York, NY 10025

This short essay, originally titled “Apologist Conception of the Productivity of All Professions”, excerpted from *Theories of Surplus Value*, the fourth volume of Karl Marx’s *Capital*.

ISBN 978-1-967751-52-5

All rights reserved. No part of this publication may be reproduced, stored in a retrieval system or transmitted in any form or by any means, electronic, mechanical, photocopying, recording or otherwise, without prior permission in writing from the Publisher.

eris.press